Annie Oakley
Saves the Day

written and illustrated by
Anna DiVito

Aladdin
New York   London   Toronto   Sydney

**Especially for Annaliese
and of course, for Erica
—A. D.**

First Aladdin edition November 2004
Text and illustrations copyright © 2004 by Anna DiVito

ALADDIN PAPERBACKS
An imprint of Simon & Schuster Children's Publishing Division
1230 Avenue of the Americas
New York, NY 10020

READY-TO-READ is a registered trademark of Simon & Schuster.

Book design by Lisa Vega
The text of this book was set in 18-Point Century Old Style.

Printed in the United States of America
12

DiVito, Anna.
Annie Oakley saves the day! / by Anna DiVito.
p. cm.—(Ready-to-read childhood of famous Americans)
Summary: While their father is away, young Annie Oakley and her brother
John help their mother during a blizzard.
ISBN 0-689-86521-X(lib. ed.) ISBN 0-689-86520-1(pbk.)
0521 LAK
1. Oakley, Annie, 1860-1926—Childhood and youth—Juvenile literature. 2. Shooters
of firearms—United States—Biography—Juvenile literature. 3. Frontier and pioneer
life—West (U.S.)—Juvenile literature. [1. Oakley, Annie, 1860-1926—Childhood and
youth. 2. Sharpshooters. 3. Women—Biography.] I. Title. II. Series: Ready-to-read
childhood of the famous Americans.
GV1157.O3D58 2004
799.3'092—dc22   2003022392

Annie and John Mosey

ran through the barnyard.

"Hurry, John! Father is loading his wagon for the mill," shouted Annie. "He will be gone all day."

"We are just in time to say good-bye," said John.

"In town I will buy our food

for the winter," said Father.

"Will you also bring us

a gift, Father?" asked John.

"Wait and see, Son.

I will be home for supper."

"We are going to build

a bird trap today," said Annie.

"Good! We will check on it

early tomorrow," said Father.

"Get along, horses!" he shouted.

As Father sped away, Annie and John met

Mother and the baby by the henhouse.

"It looks like snow," said Mother.

"I am worried about Father."

"He will make it safely home,"

said Annie. "He always does."

That afternoon, Annie and John
prepared their trap.
"Father uses corn stalks, string,
dried corn, and a stick,"
said Annie.
"Show me how," said John.

Annie broke the corn stalks into even pieces and stacked them on the ground.
The trap grew tall. It started to look like a little log house.

"Father ties the corners to make
the trap strong," she said.
"He adds a roof so the bird
will not get out."
"How does the bird get in?"
asked John.

Annie held up the stick.

She dug a path uphill to the trap.

"Father drops corn along

the path," she said.

"The stick will hold up the trap.

When the bird goes inside to eat,

it will knock down the stick

and be locked inside the trap."

John sprinkled the corn.

"Hurry, Annie, it is

getting cold," he said.

"Let's go home."

"First we must hide our trap,"

she said.

They covered the trap with leaves
and started for the cabin.

"Father will be surprised when he
finds a fat bird in the trap
in the morning," said Annie.

"I want to find a fat bird
for supper tonight," said John.

The wind howled, *EEE OOO!*

John took Annie's hand.

Snowflakes began to swirl

around them.

"Will Father be home soon, Annie?"

asked John. "It is getting dark."

"Soon," she whispered. "Soon."

That night the family ate

soup for supper.

Boom! Wind shook the windows.

Crash! A tree branch fell.

John jumped in his chair.

"Mother, I am afraid!" he cried.

"It is a blizzard," she said.

"But we are safe at home, together."

The last log burned on the fire.

"Annie," said Mother, "I need you
to get more logs from the woodpile."

Mother tied one end of a rope

to the porch post, and the other

around Annie's waist.

Annie held on to the rope.

The wind pushed and
pulled her along.
At one point Annie slipped
and dropped the firewood.

Soon Annie could not see the
cabin through the snow.
Her fingers were numb, and her
face stung. But she hung on
until she was home with the wood.

Mother threw more wood on the fire,
and the children lay down to sleep.

"Let us pray for Father on this long,
snowy night," Annie said.

She lay awake listening
to the storm.

Suddenly Annie heard horses.
"Father is home!" she cried.

Mother threw the door wide open.

Father sat on his wagon

with the horses' reigns

wrapped around his wrists.

He did not speak

or move his hands.

"Father looks frozen!" cried Annie.
"The horses must have found
their own way home."

The family carried Father inside.

Annie took his wet coat.

A bag fell from the pocket.

"Father, you remembered," said John.

"Peppermints! Thank you."

Father shivered.

"Will he be all right?"

whispered Annie.

"I hope so," said Mother.

The next morning Annie and John

crept past Father while he slept.

"A bird from our trap will cheer

Father up today," said John.

"He will feel better!"

"Hush!" whispered Annie.

"Father must rest.

   Let's hurry outside

   before we wake him."

In the woods they brushed the snow
and leaves from the trap.

"I hear it!" said Annie. "Listen!"

"What is it, Annie?"

John leaned near the trap.

"Hoy, hoy!" sang a little voice.

"It's Molly, our hen!" said John.

"It's not Molly," laughed Annie.

"It's a quail!"

Annie held up the bird.

"Father will be proud!" said John.

Annie wrapped the quail in her scarf.

"Until Father feels better,

he can count on us to help

feed the family with our traps,"

she said.

"We can do it!" said John.

"We will!" said Annie.

And they did.

Annie, later known as Annie Oakley, trapped and hunted to help her family survive many hardships.

Here is a timeline of her life:

1860	Born Phoebe Anne Mosey, in Darke County, Ohio, on August 13
1866	Jacob Mosey, Annie's father, comes home nearly frozen. Dies from pneumonia February 11
1868	Annie shoots a gun for the first time
1875	Meets Frank Butler and beats him in a shooting match on Thanksgiving Day
1876	Marries Frank Butler on August 23
1882	First uses the stage name Annie Oakley in a trick-shooting match with her husband
1885	Joins Buffalo Bill's Wild West Show
1887	Performs with Buffalo Bill's Wild West Show in England, for Queen Victoria
1901	Injured in a train wreck in North Carolina; retires from Buffalo Bill's Wild West Show
1908	Susan Mosey Shaw, Annie's mother, dies
1911	Joins the Young Buffalo Show again
1913	Gives her last show as a Young Buffalo Show star and permanently retires from performing
1926	Dies on November 3, near the family farm in Greenville, Ohio; her husband dies only 18 days later in Michigan